Original title:
Tug-of-War with Tumbling Thoughts

Copyright © 2024 Creative Arts Management OÜ
All rights reserved.

Author: Kieran Blackwood
ISBN HARDBACK: 978-9916-90-130-4
ISBN PAPERBACK: 978-9916-90-131-1

Journey through the Jumble

Amidst the twisted paths we tread,
Where laughter swirls and shadows spread.
Each step a puzzle, a riddle to chase,
Lost in the heart of this vibrant space.

Colors collide, the senses awake,
Fragrant whispers, the earth's great ache.
A map unwritten, we wander free,
In the beauty of chaos, just you and me.

Undercurrents of Emotion

Beneath the calm, the currents flow,
Hidden depths where feelings grow.
Ripples of joy, waves of despair,
A tempest brews in the quiet air.

Hearts beat softly, yet loud they cry,
In the silence, the echoes lie.
Each pulse a story, a truth unspun,
In the undercurrents, we all are one.

Echoes of Enigma

Whispered secrets in the night,
Questions wrapped in soft moonlight.
What lies behind the shadowed veil?
The search for answers, a timeless tale.

Figures dance on the edge of thought,
In puzzles woven, our minds are caught.
Mystery lingers in every gaze,
Echoes of enigma, a swirling maze.

Racing Clouds of Intellect

Thoughts like clouds race through the sky,
Ideas form, then swiftly fly.
Brilliant flashes ignite the mind,
In the storm of reason, clarity we find.

Reflections shimmer on the surface bright,
Truth emerges from the depths of night.
A dance of logic, a playful game,
In racing clouds, we're all the same.

Rippled Reflections

In tranquil waters, whispers play,
Soft shimmering echoes drift away.
Mirrored skies dancing in the blue,
Rippled reflections, old and new.

A fleeting glance at what once was,
The heart remembers, a gentle buzz.
Each wave a story, each drop a tear,
In silent depths, dreams linger near.

Sunlight flickers, a golden hue,
Shadows within, secrets ensue.
Upon the surface, stillness reigns,
Inward journeys, the soul retains.

The cycle flows, life's tender art,
Rippling moments, a healing heart.
Beneath the calm, a vibrant core,
In every ripple, we seek for more.

Cacophony of Consciousness

A thousand thoughts collide and clash,
In vibrant chaos, ideas flash.
Voices reverberate, loud and clear,
In a symphony that draws us near.

Threads of memory weave and break,
In tangled web, we dance and shake.
Chasing shadows, seeking light,
In the whirlwind, we take flight.

Questions arise like sparks in night,
In the darkness, we search for sight.
Echoes of dreams, both lost and found,
In the cacophony, truths abound.

Amidst the noise, a quiet grace,
In chaos' heart, we find our place.
Through clashing thoughts, we become whole,
In the symphony, we seek our soul.

Shattered Echoes

In empty halls where whispers dwell,
Footsteps linger, casting spells,
A laughter lost, a fading light,
Shattered echoes in the night.

Memories dance on shadowed walls,
Time's cruel hand, it gently falls,
Fragments of joy, now turned to gray,
In silent rooms, they drift away.

The Struggle of Solitude

Alone beneath the star's cold gaze,
A heart cries out in woven maze,
Walls of silence close in tight,
Yearning for the sun's soft light.

Thoughts like shadows, creeping near,
Whispers soft, yet fraught with fear,
In the depths where echoes creep,
Waking dreams that haunt my sleep.

Silken Threads of Dilemma

Woven paths of choice and chance,
Every moment, life's strange dance,
Threads of gold and shadows cast,
Tug my heart, both slow and fast.

A web of hopes, a tangled nest,
In silence lies the heart's true quest,
Each decision, a fragile thread,
Leading where the brave have tread.

Storms Beneath the Surface

Beneath the calm, the waters churn,
Hidden fury, tides that burn,
Whispers of the tempest rise,
Masking truths within the skies.

Clouds gather dark, the shadows blend,
Nature's rage, a fierce descend,
Yet in the eye, a stillness lies,
A moment caught where silence cries.

The Crossfires of Introspection

In the silence, shadows creep,
Thoughts collide, secrets deep.
A mirror shows what I can't see,
Fragments of the one I could be.

Time stands still, yet rushes by,
Whispers echo, the heart's sigh.
Questions lie in tangled thread,
Lost in words I never said.

Chasing visions, fleeting glints,
In a world where feeling hints.
Each decision, a winding road,
Carved by dreams, a heavy load.

Yet in the dark, a flicker glows,
Truth emerges, the pathway shows.
Through the crossfires, I will tread,
Finding light where I have led.

Playful Paradoxes

In a world of ups and downs,
Joy is found in fading frowns.
The sun might shine while rain may fall,
A gentle quake, a morning call.

Laughter dances on serious ground,
In the lost, the found is found.
Each twisted turn of fate's own play,
Teaches us in a curious way.

The silent shout, the loudest sigh,
With every hello, there's a goodbye.
In contradictions, we embrace,
Life's sweet chaos, a warm embrace.

So let us twirl in silent screams,
Weaving life from wildest dreams.
In paradox, we find our song,
A symphony where we belong.

Driftwood of Dilemmas

Washed ashore on thoughts adrift,
Choices linger, an endless rift.
The tide pulls back, then brings anew,
It's hard to know just what to do.

Each piece of wood tells tales unknown,
Of currents strong, and seeds once sown.
Battered lines, lost in the deep,
Worries wake when doubts don't sleep.

As storms rage on, we stand unsure,
Searching for what might feel secure.
In the wreckage, we find a spark,
Guiding lights in moments dark.

So let us gather each fragment lost,
To navigate a path, no matter the cost.
For even driftwood can craft a tale,
Of hope and strength, it shall prevail.

Cosmic Tugging

Stars collide in twilight's thread,
Binding dreams where visions spread.
In cosmic dance, we find our way,
Pulled by forces that gently sway.

Galaxies whisper in silent night,
Guiding hearts with timeless light.
Each heartbeat syncs with distant skies,
Tugging softly as the universe sighs.

Gravity holds, yet we break free,
Asteroids chart our destiny.
In the pull, a sweet embrace,
We soar through space, forever chase.

Cosmic threads weave fate's own song,
In the vastness, where we belong.
Through the tugging, we shall rise,
Exploring wonders in starry skies.

Tumbling Realms

In twilight shadows, realms collide,
Where whispers dance and secrets hide.
A cascade of stars, they gently flow,
In the tumbling night, we drift and glow.

Beneath the moon's soft silver glaze,
The world unfolds in a dreamlike haze.
Mountains sway like ancient trees,
In tumbling realms, we ride the breeze.

Time bends and shifts, a fleeting sound,
Lost in the magic, we're spellbound.
A carousel of thoughts takes flight,
In tumbling realms, we find our light.

Thoughts in Limbo

Caught between the veil of night,
And dawn's approaching warmth and light.
Thoughts in limbo, drift and sway,
In this quiet, shadowed play.

Echoes linger, undefined,
Whispers of what's left behind.
Like drifting leaves on water's sheen,
Thoughts float gently, soft and keen.

Moments frozen, yet they fade,
In the glimmer, dreams are laid.
Thoughts in limbo, soft and wide,
In this space, we seek to bide.

Wrestling with Reverie

In dreamt-up realms where shadows dwell,
I wrestle softly, caught in a spell.
Visions twist, then slip away,
In murmured thoughts, I long to stay.

With each breath, the struggle flows,
A dance of highs, a drop of lows.
In the wrestling, wisdom's gain,
Through reverie, I bear the pain.

Unseen battles spark and burn,
In the stillness, the tides do turn.
Wrestling with the fleeting mist,
In dreams' embrace, I cease to resist.

Discordant Dreams

In the night where shadows clash,
Discordant dreams begin to thrash.
Colors bleed and sounds collide,
In chaos, fears and hopes abide.

Lost in echoes, a fragmented song,
Where nothing feels quite right or wrong.
Each heartbeat is a twisted thread,
In discord's grip, we fear and tread.

Yet in the turmoil, sparks ignite,
A dance of shadows, wielding light.
Discordant dreams may fade away,
But through the noise, we'll find our way.

Waves of Contemplation

In the silence, thoughts unfold,
Echoes whisper, secrets told.
Each wave brings a fleeting spark,
Dancing shadows, light and dark.

Currents swirl beneath the night,
Restless dreams take flight in sight.
A gentle tide pulls me away,
To depths where hidden waters sway.

Reflections shimmer on the shore,
Memories linger, seeking more.
The ebb and flow, a soothing sound,
In quiet moments, peace is found.

Unraveled Mental Maze

Thoughts collide like crashing waves,
Lost in alleys, winding caves.
A flicker here, a shadow there,
In this labyrinth, I despair.

Each corner turned brings new surprise,
A haunting echo, shifting lies.
Paths obscure, they twist and turn,
Lessons fade, but yearn to learn.

Finding light is but a quest,
In tangled webs, I seek my rest.
The way ahead seems far and wide,
Yet in the dark, hope must abide.

Tidal Forces of Reflection

Moonlit waves caress the shore,
Pulling heartstrings, wanting more.
With every tide, a lesson learned,
In tranquil depths, my soul has turned.

The rhythm flows, in and out,
A dance of dreams, a whispered shout.
Each surge reveals what lies beneath,
In watery depths, I find my peace.

Ripples echo through my mind,
A gentle guide, both firm and blind.
As tides retreat, new visions bloom,
In cycles of calm, dispelling gloom.

The Storm Within

A tempest brews beneath my skin,
Whirlwinds of doubt, where to begin?
Echoes crashing, fierce and wild,
In this chaos, I'm but a child.

Lightning strikes with thoughts unchained,
A thunderous roar, yet love remains.
Waves of fear quickly arise,
Yet somewhere deep, hope never dies.

After the storm, calm waters wait,
A chance to breathe, to contemplate.
In silence found, strength will grow,
Through storms within, my spirit glows.

Pulling Strings of Perception

In shadows cast by fleeting light,
We question what we see at night.
A world adorned in mystic threads,
Each thought entwined where reason treads.

With every glance, a tale unfolds,
Of hidden truths and whispers told.
Perception's dance, a tangled weave,
In the fabric of what we believe.

The heart deciphers colors bright,
That twist and turn beyond our sight.
An echo here, a shadow there,
Each moment's spark fills empty air.

So pull the strings, and gently slide,
Through layers deep where secrets hide.
In artful ways, our minds contrive,
To find the pulse that keeps us alive.

The Currents of Chaos

Chaos flows like a restless tide,
Through tangled paths where shadows bide.
In chaos, find the untraced course,
A wild dance, a primal force.

The winds of change, they howl and mock,
Turning time like a ticking clock.
In every storm, a chance to rise,
In wildness lies the wisest guise.

Through tumultuous waves, we sail,
With heartbeats strong, we shall not pale.
Embrace the chaos, free and bold,
For in its depths, true life unfolds.

Each twist and turn, a lesson learned,
In frayed edges, wisdom burned.
From chaos blooms the sweetest grace,
A tapestry we dare to trace.

A Mind Adrift

Lost amid the sea of thought,
A restless wave that can't be caught.
Drifting gently on the breeze,
Searching for a silent ease.

In currents deep, the dreams do flow,
Each whisper soft, a gentle glow.
Yet in the spaces, fear can creep,
Awake the shadows from their sleep.

In solitude, the mind will roam,
To distant lands where thoughts call home.
A ship unmoored, it sails alone,
Across the vastness, ever known.

In every thought, a longing breath,
To grasp the life, to dance with death.
So let the tides your spirit lift,
Adrift is where we find the gift.

Balanced on the Brink

On edges sharp of folly's choice,
We hear the whispers of our voice.
A fragile line, a heart's demand,
To find the strength to stand, to stand.

Each moment hangs, a fleeting thread,
As fears arise, as courage bled.
With balanced feet, we dance the night,
A spark of hope, a flickering light.

In every pause, a risk we take,
The ground beneath begins to quake.
Yet forward's call, it pulls us near,
To chase the dreams we once held dear.

So let us waltz upon the brink,
With every heartbeat, dare to think.
For in the balance, joy and pain,
We find the wisdom we regain.

Labyrinth of Doubts

In shadows deep, where whispers grow,
The paths twist tight, I feel the throe.
Each step I take, I wonder still,
What truths are veiled, what bends the will.

A silent voice stirs in my chest,
With echoes where my fears find rest.
This maze of thoughts, so hard to chart,
Leaves me adrift, yet clings to heart.

The walls they shift, the light will fade,
As questions rise like ghosts in shade.
I grasp at threads, so thin, so frail,
In this vast space where doubts prevail.

Yet hope ignites a flicker bright,
A beacon firm within the night.
Though tangled paths lead far and wide,
Each turn reveals a deeper guide.

Whirlwinds of Reflection

In bending winds, my thoughts take flight,
Each gust a chance to seek the light.
Clouds swirl around, a dance so wild,
Bringing dreams of times I've reconciled.

The past like leaves, they whirl and play,
Tracing paths of who I've been each day.
In moments lost, my heart recalls,
Life's fleeting shades through transient halls.

The storms may rage, the skies may weep,
Yet in their heart, a promise keep.
For in the chaos, clarity glows,
Wisdom's seeds the tempest sows.

So I embrace the storm's embrace,
A swirling dance, a sacred space.
In whirlwinds bright, I find my truth,
A journey marked with age and youth.

The Mind's Tug

A pull within, a ceaseless thread,
Thoughts like shadows dance in my head.
Each whisper calls, a silent plea,
A tug of war, it's me and me.

What path to take, the right or wrong?
This inner fight feels endless, long.
Moments of peace, then doubt's cruel jest,
What lays ahead, I can only guess.

The battle brews beneath the skin,
With every breath, the noise, the din.
Yet in the struggle, strength is found,
In quiet depths, I'm safe, I'm sound.

So I will stand, despite the strife,
Embracing all parts of this life.
For in the tug of thought and might,
I forge my way from dark to light.

Fraying Threads of Thought

As threads unwind, they tangle tight,
In woven patterns, lost from sight.
Delicate strands of woven past,
Hold secrets whispering, fading fast.

Each thought a stitch, a memory spun,
A tapestry of all I've done.
Yet fragile seams begin to break,
Revealing paths this mind can take.

With gentle hands, I trace the weave,
Rekindling dreams I dare to believe.
Though frayed and worn, I'll mend with care,
Embracing every joy and dare.

So here I stand, threads in my palm,
Finding solace in the calm.
For though they fray, my heart's intent,
Is to weave anew, unbroken, bent.

Conflicted Echoes

Deep within, the whispers clash,
A haunting song that fades to ash.
Thoughts like shadows dance and play,
In the silence of the fray.

Voices pull in different ways,
Lost in dark and endless maze.
Heart and mind, they intertwine,
Searching for a spark, a sign.

Hope and doubt, forever near,
Chasing light, yet gripped by fear.
Echoes of a life once bright,
Fade to gray, lost in the night.

Juggling Shadows

Fingers deftly toss and play,
Balancing the night and day.
Shadows flicker, twist and bend,
Secrets kept, they never end.

Each illusion, a fragile thread,
Life's a stage where dreams are fed.
Caught in games of hide and seek,
Silent screams and hearts that peek.

Masks we wear and roles we last,
Juggling truths in shadows cast.
Yet beneath the fleeting light,
Lies the dawn beyond the night.

The Tugging Mind

Thoughts entangle, pull apart,
Threads of reason, strings of heart.
In the storm, the quiet cries,
As I search for hidden lies.

Questions swirl like endless breeze,
Hopes and fears that never ease.
Each decision weighs like stone,
Craving solace, yet alone.

Time eludes the grasping hand,
Waves of doubt upon the sand.
Yet within the storm I find,
A flicker in the tugging mind.

Waging Inner Wars

Battles fought in silence deep,
Voices rise where shadows creep.
Every choice, a line of fire,
Fueling dreams or dousing desire.

Conflicted loyalties collide,
In the depths where fears reside.
Waging wars no one can see,
Yet they shape the soul of me.

Torn between the light and dark,
Fighting fetters, leaving marks.
In the chaos, strength I find,
Waging on, the war of mind.

Mind's Tension Dance

In shadows where the worries seethe,
A rhythm pulses, sharp and brief.
Thoughts collide like thunder's crash,
In silence, dreams begin to clash.

The heartbeats skip, the mind's ablaze,
In every step, a twisted maze.
Each breath a struggle, whispered sighs,
In the dance of doubt, the spirit lies.

Twisting, turning, seeking peace,
In the chaos, I find release.
Light breaks through the darkest shade,
In tension's grip, my fears cascade.

Yet in this dance, I come alive,
A spark ignites, a will to strive.
With every spin, I face the chance,
To find my strength in tension's dance.

Fractured Reveries

Dreams like glass, they shatter bright,
Reflecting hopes in fractured light.
Each piece a story, lost but near,
In broken whispers, truths appear.

Silent echoes, past's embrace,
Memories shifting, time's own race.
Shards of longing scatter wide,
In fractured dreams, I seek to hide.

The canvas splinters, color bleeds,
From bitter roots, new life proceeds.
In every crack, a tale unfolds,
Lost reveries clinging to the cold.

Yet through the shards, a beauty gleams,
In every fracture, life redeems.
These shattered visions intertwine,
Fractured reveries, once divine.

Torn Threads of Reflection

In the fabric of the mind's expanse,
Torn threads weave a vast expanse.
Every stitch a moment lost,
In reflection's mirror, I pay the cost.

Silken strands of joy and pain,
Woven tightly, yet they strain.
Caught in time's relentless weave,
In torn threads, I learn to believe.

The patterns shift, the colors fade,
Yet in this tapestry, I'm made.
With every tear, a tale unfolds,
In reflection's heart, the truth beholds.

Amidst the wreckage, I discern,
From every loss, a chance to learn.
In the torn threads, I find my way,
A guiding light in disarray.

Aces and Embers

In the silence, whispers spark,
Aces played in shadows dark.
Fires flicker, bright then dim,
A song of chance on a fragile whim.

Embers dance in the cool night air,
Each flicker holds a secret prayer.
Let the cards fall where they may,
In the gamble, I choose to stay.

With every hand, the stakes arise,
In the game of fate, we paralyze.
Yet in the risk, there's bold delight,
Aces and embers, fate ignites.

So let the night unfold its charm,
In every loss, I find my balm.
For in this play, life's essence glows,
Aces and embers, where my heart knows.

Fractured Reflections

In the mirror, shadows play,
Whispers of the light decay.
Shattered dreams in pieces lay,
Glimmers of a brighter day.

Faces change, they blend and blur,
Echoes fade, they softly stir.
Fragments lost, we reach and purr,
Seeking truth in what was sure.

Tangled thoughts in silent night,
Searching for that guiding light.
Cracks reveal the hidden sights,
Wounds remind us of the fight.

In the shards, a path we find,
Healing slowly, yet so blind.
Fractured hearts can still be kind,
In reflections intertwined.

Twists of the Mind

In a labyrinth of thought,
Dualities are dearly fought.
Winding paths we never sought,
Lost connections, always caught.

Ideas spiral, twist, and twine,
Between the chaos, hope will shine.
A dance of reason, so divine,
The maze of mind, a secret sign.

Words collide in mental games,
Whispers echo, none to blame.
Evolving patterns, none the same,
In this space, we will reclaim.

Dilemmas rise and overlap,
Deep within a mental map.
Chasing shadows, hear the clap,
As we weave our tangled chap.

Battle of the Brainwaves

A storm brews in silent night,
Thoughts collide, a fierce insight.
Waves crash hard, a daunting fight,
Mind and heart in frayed delight.

Echoes of the past arise,
Challenging the quiet skies.
In this clash, no one is wise,
Stormy fates and heavy sighs.

Fractured pulses, beats align,
Ideas pulse, and fears intertwine.
In the chaos, truths may shine,
A battle fought in shifting line.

Yet in the storm, we learn to bend,
Finding peace as thoughts descend.
In the struggle, we can mend,
A journey forged, no need to pretend.

The Pull of Dissonance

Notes collide in sharp refrain,
Harmony begins to wane.
Tension builds, a subtle strain,
In this dance of joy and pain.

Dissonance, a haunting call,
Echoes through the empty hall.
Crimson whispers, rise and fall,
In this chaos, we stand tall.

Unsettled minds, they sway and twist,
Lost in shadows, moments missed.
In the clamor, sparks persist,
A gentle heart that can't resist.

Yet through the discord, peace breaks free,
Melodies of what could be.
Finding balance, a symphony,
In the pull of dissonance, we see.

The Balance of Shadows

In twilight's grasp, shadows play,
Dancing softly, night meets day.
Whispers linger in the air,
Echoes fading, unaware.

Branches stretch, a silent plea,
Casting forms for all to see.
The light retreats, a gentle sigh,
As coal-black dreams begin to fly.

Time wavers on the edge of night,
Shivering stars, a distant light.
Each moment teeters on its brink,
In the balance, shadows think.

Yet in darkness, there is peace,
A quiet breath, a sweet release.
In the void, find your tomorrow,
Amidst the balance, shed your sorrow.

Lattice of Lament

Threads of sorrow weave the night,
Tangled tales of lost delight.
Each stitch tells a story old,
Of memories once bright and bold.

In the heart of a weeping willow,
Lies the echo of a hollow.
Whispered secrets, soft and low,
In this lattice, feelings flow.

Petals fall, like tears from grace,
Marking time with gentle trace.
Fragile dreams in soft decay,
Each lament singing their way.

Yet through the gloom, a spark ignites,
Hope glimmers in new found heights.
Within the weave, a strength to bear,
The lattice holds a love laid bare.

Strained Silhouettes

Figures dance in the twilight haze,
Fleeting forms in a smoky gaze.
Each silhouette, a ghostly spark,
Fading softly into the dark.

Hope and fear, a tight embrace,
Strained emotions in every space.
Beneath the moon's watchful eye,
Life's fragile shadows flicker nigh.

Time's cruel hand bends the light,
Softer edges fade from sight.
Yet within the darkest breath,
Strains of life deny their death.

Hold on tight to every thread,
In this dance, the light is shed.
Strained silhouettes may bend and break,
But resilience thrives with every ache.

Moonlit Murmurs

Beneath the moon's soft, silken glow,
Secrets rise, like whispers slow.
Each murmur carries tales untold,
Of ancient nights and dreams of gold.

Stars align in a cosmic tune,
Lighting paths beneath the moon.
Gentle laughter, echoes clear,
In the stillness, hearts draw near.

Every glance, a fleeting touch,
In the silence, we share so much.
Promises linger on the breeze,
Wrapped in night, they softly tease.

Moonlit murmurs, sweet and rare,
Carry hopes upon the air.
In the dark, our spirits soar,
Finding peace forevermore.

Inner Landscapes in Flux

In the quiet dusk of thought,
Waves of change roll softly in.
Mountains rise and fall like dreams,
Shifting sands, where thoughts begin.

Shadows dance on inner skies,
Light and dark in constant play.
Brushstrokes of a restless mind,
Canvas brightening the gray.

Moments flicker, then dissolve,
Time a river, swift and deep.
Caught in currents, we evolve,
Secrets that our hearts will keep.

Yet in this flux, a spark ignites,
Hope emerges from the fray.
In the chaos, we find peace,
Guiding us along the way.

Mind's Battlefield

Clashing thoughts in endless night,
Echoes of a fierce debate.
Wounds of doubt cut through the fog,
Who will rise, and who will wait?

Embers smolder in the dark,
Fury brews beneath the skin.
Enemies, a bitter mark,
Fighting battles deep within.

Yet, from chaos, strength can grow,
Out of strife, new visions gleam.
Voices whisper, seeds we sow,
Cultivate the fiercest dream.

Victory is not one side,
But unity in life's great score.
Together, they will turn the tide,
In peace they'll learn to soar.

Chaotic Whispers

Whispers flutter in the air,
Thoughts collide like scattered leaves.
Fractured echoes seek repair,
In the chaos, hope believes.

Fleeting shadows, flickers bright,
Tangled threads of joy and woe.
In the tumult, search for light,
Trust the path our hearts bestow.

Every whisper tells a tale,
Woven deep in fractured mind.
Through the storm, we learn to sail,
New horizons yet to find.

In this dance of scattered sound,
Harmony can start to rise.
From the chaos, we are bound,
In our whispers, wisdom lies.

The Struggle Within

Within the depths, a silent fight,
Voices clash, their echoes swell.
Stars and shadows spark the night,
In the depths where secrets dwell.

Chained by fears, yet thirsting free,
Battles rage beneath the skin.
Finding strength in vulnerability,
Embracing all that lies within.

Mountains rise and valleys fall,
Every step is carved in stone.
Through the struggle, we stand tall,
Learning how to claim our own.

In the quiet, courage grows,
With each tear shed, we are whole.
Guided by the heart's soft glow,
Discovering the strength of soul.

Juggling Shadows of Tomorrow

In twilight's grip, the shadows play,
A dance of dreams that drift away.
With every toss, a hope takes flight,
Yet fears remain, concealed from sight.

The juggler's hands, both deft and sure,
Balance the weight of dreams unsure.
Each shadow flickers, whispers clear,
Of paths yet formed, of love and fear.

A fleeting glimpse of what could be,
In every jolt, a memory.
A chance to grasp, to hold, to keep,
As night descends, and dreams take leap.

So watch them dance, those shadows bold,
Stories of tomorrow, yet untold.
In twilight's embrace, we find our way,
Through juggling shadows, night and day.

Echoes from the Abyss

From depths unknown, a whisper calls,
An echo rolls through darkened halls.
Forgotten tales of a time long past,
Resonate through shadows cast.

The abyss stirs with secrets deep,
In silent corners where lost thoughts creep.
Each haunting sound, a tale concealed,
A truth so raw, yet never revealed.

Taken by currents of the unseen,
Drifting between the fierce and serene.
The echo rises, then fades away,
Yet leaves its mark, a price to pay.

Listen closely, let the silence speak,
In the abyss, the strong stay weak.
For every echo, a heart will know,
The mysteries in the depths below.

Wrestling with Tomorrow's Ghosts

In the stillness of the night, I fight,
With shadows born of day and light.
Ghosts of dreams that haunt my mind,
A canvas blurred, no peace to find.

They whisper doubts, they tug at hope,
A battle fierce, with no clear scope.
Each specter dances on the edge,
Pulling me close, to break my pledge.

Yet in this struggle, strength unfolds,
A fire within, a heart so bold.
For every ghost that tries to claim,
A piece of me, ignites a flame.

Wrestling shadows, fighting them back,
With every strike, I pave my track.
Tomorrow's ghosts may linger still,
But I will rise, I bend, I will.

The Duality of Dreams

In daylight bright, our dreams take form,
As hope ignites, a rising storm.
Yet in the dark, they shift and change,
A paradox that feels so strange.

They pull us high, then drop us low,
A dance of light, a game of woe.
In waking hours, they seem so clear,
But in the night, they disappear.

Each dream a bridge from here to there,
A longing quest, a whispered dare.
We chase and pause, we feel the fight,
In duality, we find our light.

Embrace the night and greet the dawn,
For in this dance, we carry on.
The duality of dreams will guide,
Through every ebb, with hope as tide.

Chasing Fragmented Thoughts

In shadowed corners, whispers cling,
Fragments shift like drifting sand.
Voices echo in the silent ring,
Caught between dreams we can't understand.

Thoughts scatter like leaves in the breeze,
Fleeting glimpses of what might be.
They dance and twirl with effortless ease,
Leaving traces of possibility.

Through the labyrinth of my mind,
I chase the pieces, lost and free.
In the chaos, clarity I find,
A tapestry of the unseen me.

Yet as I grasp, they slip away,
The puzzle won't fit in the light.
In this chase, I slowly sway,
Chasing shadows into the night.

Ebbing Ideas

Ideas flow like waves at sea,
Rising high, then sinking low.
In the tide, what will be free?
Thoughts cascade, then overflow.

Moments grasped then let to fade,
The rush of brilliance starts to wane.
In shadows cast, ambitions laid,
A tide that calls, yet yields to rain.

With shifting sands beneath my toes,
I reach for dreams, but they recede.
The heart yearns for what it knows,
Ebbing ideas planted like seed.

Yet in this dance of loss and gain,
I find solace in what remains.
With every ebb, a lesson learned,
In the quiet surf, my soul is burned.

Constellations of Confusion

Stars above flicker, whisper doubt,
Constellations shift in hazy skies.
In their patterns, I search about,
For clarity lost in swirling lies.

A map of chaos, bright yet absurd,
Guiding thoughts that wander far.
In the silence, not a single word,
Yet light within each fading star.

Threads of midnight weave and tangle,
A fabric stitched with faded dreams.
In confusion's embrace, I dangle,
Mapping out my silent screams.

Yet still I stare, embracing night,
Finding wonder in the vast unknown.
In these constellations, lost in flight,
I find the beauty in the wandering alone.

A Symphony of Distraction

Notes of chaos fill the air,
Each sound a fleeting, playful tease.
A symphony of thoughts laid bare,
Drowning in the din of unease.

Melodies crash like ocean waves,
Pulling me from focus's shore.
In each distraction, madness raves,
As concentration drifts, unsure.

Yet in this noise, a rhythm caught,
Competing harmonies collide.
From scattered tunes, a lesson taught,
In disarray, new paths do bide.

Through dissonance, I find a theme,
A song that rises from the fray.
In this symphony, an echo gleams,
A dance through chaos, come what may.

Threads of Tension

In shadows deep, the silence holds,
A whispering breeze, a story unfolds.
Moments teeter on the edge of fate,
Each heartbeat counts, it's never too late.

Tightrope walkers on a fragile line,
Every decision, a chance to shine.
With every glance, a spark ignites,
An endless dance of fears and rights.

The binding strings of hope and dread,
Weaving tales of what lies ahead.
In every choice, a weight so grand,
Life's intricate patterns, by chance, we stand.

Yet through the storm, we stand, we sway,
Finding strength in the fray each day.
For in the tension, beauty is spun,
A tapestry bright, where we all are one.

An Odyssey within the Mind

Through corridors of thought, I roam,
Past echoes of dreams that feel like home.
Mountains rise, and valleys fall,
In the landscape of the mind, I hear the call.

Words like rivers, flowing free,
Carving paths of what could be.
Visions pulse like distant stars,
Guiding me through life's avatars.

Whispers of wisdom dance in the air,
Lessons learned, stories laid bare.
Emotions ebb like the moon's tide,
In this odyssey, I shall confide.

Wrapped in thoughts, both wild and tame,
I embark on adventures, sans any shame.
For every thought's a journey bright,
An odyssey in the depth of night.

Whimsical Warnings

In the garden where shadows play,
Frolicking thoughts begin to sway.
A butterfly lands on a dandelion,
Whispering secrets of the lion.

The clock ticks loud, but time stands still,
Chasing dreams, we bend to will.
A jester's grin hides deep despair,
A whimsical warning hangs in the air.

The moon winks down with playful light,
Guiding lost souls through the night.
Step lightly, dear, on paths unknown,
For every jest, a truth is sown.

Laughter echoes, sweet and bright,
Yet shadows linger, out of sight.
Heed the whims, the signs, the calls,
In this dance where laughter falls.

The Weight of Uncertainty

Laden with questions, the heart does sigh,
In turbulent seas, we must rely.
Navigating through the foggy haze,
Seeking answers in a complex maze.

With every step, a choice to weigh,
Ghosts of doubt lead us astray.
The future's pull, a heavy chain,
Yet still we rise through joy and pain.

Hope shines bright like a flickering flame,
Guiding us through the depths of the game.
Yet questions linger, shadows cast,
In the dance of present, future, past.

Embrace the unknown, the path we tread,
For in the weight, new dreams are bred.
With every heartbeat, we learn to see,
The beauty within uncertainty.

Echoing Hesitations

In the shadows, whispers dwell,
Where doubts in silence weave their spell.
Each heartbeat drifts as time unspools,
Caught in the web of unspoken rules.

Moments linger, lost in thought,
Fragments of truth that life forgot.
In the stillness, echoes call,
Reminders of fears that softly fall.

Treading lightly on fragile ground,
Searching for solace that can't be found.
Every pause, a chance to breathe,
Yet in the silence, more to seethe.

But still we stand, eyes open wide,
Facing the waves that ebb and glide.
With hesitations, we find our way,
Through echoing doubts of yesterday.

Tides of Time

Time flows like a river's stream,
Washing away our hopes and dreams.
Each wave a moment, a fleeting grace,
Carving our path in this vast space.

The sun sets low as shadows grow,
Casting reflections of all we know.
With every dawn, new chances rise,
Yet, like the tide, they fade and die.

In the swell of years, we find our place,
Wrapped in the arms of nature's embrace.
Yet memories linger, like grains of sand,
Touching our hearts with a gentle hand.

We ride the current, we dance in the flow,
Embracing the change, we learn to grow.
For in the tides of time, we see,
The beauty of life, a vast sea.

Tenuous Threads of Insight

In the web of thoughts, we find our way,
Through fragile strands that lead astray.
Each insight flickers, a candle's glow,
Illuminating paths we cannot know.

Careful we tread on this fragile ground,
Listening for wisdom in silence found.
Threads pull tight, then unravel slow,
As we ponder the things we do not show.

Questions arise in the depths of night,
Challenging shadows, seeking the light.
With tenuous threads, we weave our fate,
Recording the echoes of thoughts innate.

Yet through the chaos, we gather strength,
Finding the depth in every length.
With insights gained, we start to see,
The tapestry of our own journey.

Flickers of Despair

In the quiet, shadows creep,
Flickers of despair begin to seep.
A heart once bright, now dulled by pain,
Seeking solace, yet bound in chains.

Whispers echo in the dark of night,
Memories taunt like a fading light.
Each breath a struggle, a silent plea,
Longing for hope, yearning to be free.

Days blend together, a weary haze,
Lost in the grip of a dense malaise.
Yet still a spark, within us lies,
A flicker of courage that never dies.

In the depth of despair, we learn to fight,
Finding strength in the heart's soft light.
Flickers may fade, but they'll always spark,
Guiding us through the depths so dark.

Lost in a Mental Labyrinth

Wandering paths of tangled thought,
Each turn leads to battles fought.
Echoes whisper secrets deep,
In shadows where lost visions creep.

Climbing walls of doubt and fear,
Every corner draws me near.
Frayed edges of a once clear mind,
In this maze, clarity's hard to find.

Labyrinthine paths entwine,
In the dark, I search for signs.
Hours turn to days of strife,
Seeking walls that once held life.

Yet in the chaos, I must trust,
Finding peace amidst the rust.
Through the haze, a light might shine,
Guiding me from the line divine.

The War of Whims

Whispers bounce from thought to thought,
In this dance, each whim is caught.
Minds collide in playful feuds,
Each idea strutting in its moods.

Fickle hearts wage battles bold,
Trading stories, new and old.
Curious twists in the air do play,
Fleeting visions drift away.

Imagination sparks a fight,
Pushing dreams into the light.
Over realms of make-believe,
In this war, we learn to weave.

The victor's crown is never clear,
With every laughter, every tear.
Together we embrace the strife,
Savoring the whimsy of life.

Searching for Grounding

In a world that spins too fast,
Questions linger, shadows cast.
Feet that long to feel the earth,
Yearning for a moment's worth.

Wanderlust leads me on a quest,
Seeking solace, yearning rest.
Nature's touch, a gentle balm,
In its presence, I find calm.

Breath by breath, I start to see,
Roots entwined, embracing me.
Balance found in simple sights,
Stars that shine through quiet nights.

In every rustling whispering leaf,
A binding force beyond belief.
Grounded in this cosmic dance,
Finding peace in every chance.

Flickering Comets of Thought

Shooting stars across the sky,
Ideas flare and swiftly fly.
A flicker here, then gone from sight,
In the vastness of the night.

Each comet leaves a trail behind,
Glimmers of the curious mind.
Chasing thoughts like fireflies,
Illuminating hidden sighs.

In the darkness, brilliance glows,
From whispers where the wild wind blows.
Capturing moments, capturing light,
Fleeting visions take to flight.

Yet in the chase, sparks may fall,
Remnants of a journey, small.
Though they fade, they leave a mark,
Guiding dreams through the dark.

Fraying Edges of Clarity

In shadows cast by fleeting light,
Words tremble, lost, in quiet night.
Thoughts wander on a fragile thread,
While reason's voice begins to shred.

A tapestry of doubt unfurls,
Each truth a pearl that softly swirls.
Yet hope remains in muted glow,
A whisper through the ebb and flow.

In fractured moments, joy and pain,
Turn clarity to soft refrain.
The edges fray, yet beauty weaves,
In tangled paths, our heart believes.

Contested Dreams Unraveled

In realms where wishes dare to soar,
Some find the key, while others bore.
Dreams clash and meld, a war of sprites,
As hearts contend through darker nights.

Threads of ambition tug and strain,
Each spark ignites a stubborn flame.
Through silent cries and hidden sighs,
We chart the course of unseen skies.

With every step, the visions blur,
As doubts arise, and hopes concur.
Yet still we chase those fading beams,
In tangled webs of restless dreams.

The Clash of Silent Beats

In silent halls where echoes dwell,
A rhythm pulses, hard to quell.
In stillness, whispers come alive,
Creating sounds in which we strive.

The heart's own drum, a subtle fight,
With every thud, we seek the light.
A dance unseen yet deeply felt,
In every pause, emotions melt.

Synchronized, yet worlds apart,
Each beat a tether to the heart.
Though silence reigns, we find our way,
In clashes deep, we learn to play.

Entwined in Distracted Symphony

A melody of thoughts collide,
In harmony, we often hide.
Strings of time pull tight, then fray,
In quiet chaos, we lose our way.

Notes scatter like leaves in a storm,
Each sound a shape, each shape a form.
Through tangled measures, shadows gleam,
In fractured chords, we chase the dream.

Yet still, we dance through disarray,
With every wrong, we learn to play.
Entwined, we weave our hesitant song,
In distracted symphony, we belong.

Paintbrush of Paradox

With colors bright and shadows deep,
I wield a brush where secrets seep.
The canvas cries, a silent plea,
In strokes that form what cannot be.

Each hue reveals a different tale,
A clash of paths where dreams prevail.
Yet in the chaos, beauty finds,
A thread that weaves through hearts and minds.

A swirl of joy, a splash of pain,
In every stroke, the heart's disdain.
Creating worlds where none exist,
In paradox, the truth persists.

So let the colors dance and play,
In vivid shades, they find their way.
The paintbrush whispers, soft yet bold,
In every heart, a story told.

The Tug of Uncertainty

In shadows cast by fleeting dreams,
We linger long 'neath starlit beams.
A push and pull, the heart's own fight,
In silent echoes of the night.

Will fate align, or drift apart?
Each question weighs upon the heart.
With every step, a choice is made,
In wavering light, our hopes cascade.

The calm before the storm arrives,
In doubt's embrace, our spirit strives.
Yet in the chaos, strength is found,
In every doubt, a heart unbound.

So trust the path where shadows fall,
Embrace the fear, it's worth it all.
For in the dance of chance we see,
The beauty in uncertainty.

Balancing on the Edge of Now

On the precipice, we pause and sway,
Between the past and the light of day.
A moment holds the world inside,
In breaths we take, we learn to glide.

Each heartbeat echoes, time does blend,
In fragile grace where thoughts suspend.
We dance on edges, sharp yet true,
In whispers soft, the world anew.

With every choice, a step we gain,
Yet teetering close, we feel the strain.
A journey's path we carve with care,
In fleeting seconds, dreams laid bare.

So hold the now in trembling hands,
As life unfolds, like shifting sands.
For in the edge, we find our place,
A balance found, an endless grace.

Whirls of Discordant Whimsy

In tangled threads of laughter's sound,
The whimsy spins, a joy unbound.
With colors bright and dances light,
We waltz through dreams, taking flight.

A jester's hat upon our head,
In playful antics, laughter spread.
Each note a twist, each turn a glance,
In discord found, we learn to dance.

The whims may clash, but hearts align,
In chaos bright, a grand design.
For in the wild, the strange, the free,
We find the truth of you and me.

So let us twirl through night and day,
In whirls of joy, we'll find our way.
For life's a jest, a comic play,
In whimsy's hand, we dare to stay.

The Pendulum's Dance

In shadows cast by ticking hands,
The whispers of time make their demands.
Each swing reveals the paths we tread,
A silent dance where fears are fed.

Moments shift like grains of sand,
Between the future and what's unplanned.
With every pulse, a heartbeat skips,
In life's embrace, the pendulum flips.

We walk the line of what's begun,
From dusk till dawn, the day is spun.
In every tick, a chance to learn,
Embrace the shifts, let passion burn.

So sway with time, let worries cease,
In the pendulum's dance, find peace.
With each return, a cycle meets,
A rhythm sweet where time retreats.

Serpentines in the Mind

Thoughts like serpents twist and wind,
Beneath the surface, truth we find.
They curl and coil, a tangled thread,
In shadows deep, where fears are bred.

In silent whispers, secrets lie,
Through labyrinths, they stretch and sigh.
Each turn reveals what's left behind,
A journey mapped in the mind unkind.

Yet through the dark, a spark can glow,
In serpentines, we learn to grow.
With every twist, a chance to see,
The hidden paths to set us free.

So navigate with gentle grace,
In your own thoughts, find your place.
Embrace the journey, face the grind,
For in the maze, peace you may find.

Blooms of Clarity

In gardens where the stillness breathes,
Awakening blooms dance in the leaves.
Petals unfurl, a vibrant sight,
Revealing truths in morning light.

Each color speaks, a story shared,
Of heart's desires and dreams declared.
In fragrant hues, our souls align,
In every bloom, a hope divine.

As waters flow and seasons change,
In nature's grasp, we rearrange.
With every petal that falls away,
We find our voice, we learn to sway.

So honor the blooms that grace our path,
In every moment, embrace their math.
For in their beauty, we see what's clear,
A tapestry woven, held so dear.

Crossing the Chasm

On the edge of a daunting divide,
Where shadows linger and fears abide.
We gather courage, hearts aligned,
To leap the void, the path defined.

Each breath a whisper, a step we take,
In twilight's glow, our spirits awake.
The chasm calls, a siren's song,
We find our strength where we belong.

Through trembling hands and racing hearts,
With faith ignited, we play our parts.
For on the other side awaits,
A world of wonder and opened gates.

So take the leap, let doubts fall away,
In every chasm, find your way.
With courage fierce, the gap we span,
Crossing the chasm, we rise as one.

The Siege of Serenity

In a garden of dreams, peace dons her crown,
Yet storms rise swiftly, threatening to drown.
The walls of calm shake, the moorings strain,
But hearts find strength, to lessen the pain.

A whisper of hope floats soft in the air,
As shadows retreat, dispelled by a prayer.
The sun bursts through clouds, a radiant beam,
Restoring the faith we weave in our dream.

Yet soldiers of doubt lurk beyond the gate,
Surveying the land, they plot and they wait.
But courage ignites, a fire anew,
In the face of despair, brightly it grew.

So stand we united, through night and through day,
Defending our fortress, come what may.
With love as our armor, we'll never surrender,
This Siege of Serenity, our hearts will remember.

Wrestling with Whispers

In the quiet of night, secrets abound,
Whispers of doubt, they circle around.
Fingers dance lightly, tracing the scars,
Echoes of battles, beneath distant stars.

Fleeting thoughts tangle, a web finely spun,
Dancing like shadows, then quickly they're gone.
Yet in the stillness, a strength starts to rise,
Butterflies flutter, unyielding as ties.

With each tender whisper, I grapple and sway,
Measuring fears in the light of the day.
But clarity comes, with a gentle embrace,
In wrestling with whispers, I find my true place.

So let the winds howl, let the echoes scream,
For within this struggle, I forge my own dream.
With each tender triumph, my spirit will soar,
In wrestling with whispers, I'm learning to roar.

Flickering Flames of Clarity

In the dark of confusion, small flickers ignite,
Dancing like fireflies, banishing night.
Each spark a thought, illuminating the mind,
In the heart of the storm, true visions we find.

Like candles in windows, they beckon and glow,
Leading us onwards, through valleys of woe.
With flickering flames, our path becomes clear,
Each flame whispers softly, "Your truth is right here."

We gather the embers, nurturing light,
Kindling the warmth, and chasing the fright.
For every small flame, there's courage inside,
As we journey through shadows, with hope as our guide.

In this dance of awareness, we rise from the ash,
Flickering flames of clarity, bold and brash.
Together we steadfastly fan the bright glow,
Illuminating pathways, where love's rivers flow.

Shadows of Uncertainty

In the pantheon of doubt, shadows creep low,
Stitching together the tales that we sow.
Each murmur a question, as fog drapes the day,
Uncertainty's cloak, we wear it in gray.

Yet soft are the moments, where silence unfolds,
In the heart of the mystery, new courage beholds.
Embracing the unknown, we learn how to be,
Navigating through shadows, setting our spirits free.

With every footstep, a choice to be made,
The rhythm of life, in this dance unafraid.
For every lost path, new trails intertwine,
In the tapestry woven, our fates align.

So step into twilight, let shadows entwine,
For through uncertainty's veil, the stars brightly shine.
With hearts wide open, we shall roam with grace,
Conquering the shadows, one challenge we face.

Bound by Unseen Forces

In shadows deep, our fates entwine,
Invisible threads, a secret sign.
Through whispers soft, we find our way,
Bound by forces that seldom sway.

With every step, a silent pull,
A dance of souls, both full and dull.
In stillness lies the heart's request,
To seek the truth, to find our rest.

Yet doubts may rise, like fog at dawn,
Challenging the bonds we've drawn.
But through the haze, we choose to steer,
Embracing paths that draw us near.

Together, we face the veiled embrace,
Carved by time, a sacred space.
With every heartbeat, every glance,
We navigate this cosmic dance.

Rippled Waves of Hesitation

In quiet pools, the ripples play,
Echoes of thoughts that tend to sway.
A single doubt can stir the sea,
Creating waves that long to be.

As choices loom, and time stands still,
The heart flutters against the will.
Each ripple holds a voice of fear,
That whispers softly, 'Stay right here.'

But courage shines, a beacon bright,
To pierce the veil of endless night.
With every choice, the waves subside,
Revealing paths we've long denied.

In splashes fierce, we learn to flow,
Embracing tides that ebb and grow.
For with each wave that meets the shore,
We find the strength to seek and soar.

Fickle Flames of Thought

A flicker spark, a transient glow,
Ideas dance, then ebb, then flow.
In restless minds, the flames ignite,
Chasing shadows in the night.

Thoughts leap high, then dim to gray,
Fickle as the winds of May.
In fleeting moments, brilliance shines,
But soon retreats to tangled lines.

We chase the fire, yet feel the chill,
Yearning for a greater thrill.
But every flame, though bright, may fade,
Leaving whispers of dreams delayed.

So cherish sparks, both brave and meek,
For in their glow, our truths may peek.
Through winds of change, we stand and wait,
Guided by the whims of fate.

The Weight of Wandering Minds

In gardens lush, our thoughts collide,
A heavy heart, a restless tide.
We drift through dreams, both lost and found,
Yet long for peace, a solid ground.

With burdens borne of endless quest,
Our minds crave solace, yet know no rest.
Each thought a weight, on fragile wings,
A symphony of what life brings.

In twilight's hush, we seek the stars,
Mapping paths through dreams and scars.
We wander on, through tangled skies,
Searching for truth with desperate sighs.

But in the weight, we glean the light,
For every shadow sparks our flight.
With every step, we learn to find,
The grace that hides in wandering minds.

Fleeting Fragments

Whispers of dreams linger in the air,
Scattered like petals, light and rare.
Moments collide, then swiftly depart,
Leaving soft echoes within the heart.

Time dances lightly, teasing the mind,
Each fleeting fragment, a treasure to find.
We chase the sunlight, we yearn to hold,
But grasping at shadows, we watch them fold.

In pages of memory, some words remain,
Like grains of sand caught in life's vast plane.
We gather the pieces, we try to be whole,
Yet slip like water, ungraspable soul.

Yet in each fragment, the beauty reveals,
A tapestry woven with hopes and ideal.
So cherish the moments, let them fly free,
For even in fleeting, we find our true glee.

Shifting Sands of Thought

Ideas drift softly on winds that are strong,
Like shifting sands, where they all belong.
One moment they settle, then scatter away,
Leaving behind traces of what they might say.

The dunes of perception rise high and then fall,
An endless landscape where reason stands tall.
We navigate currents, both fierce and profound,
In this realm of thoughts, where peace can be found.

In stillness we ponder, what lies just beyond,
The ever-changing patterns, the mind's gentle bond.
With each ebb and flow, we grasp at the unknown,
Sculpting our visions from thoughts overgrown.

So let us embrace this vast, shifting land,
Where ideas like grains slip right through our hand.
For in every moment, a new path we plot,
In the tides of our thoughts, may we find what we sought.

The Tightrope of Turmoil

Balanced on whispers, where chaos ignites,
A tightrope of turmoil, a dance with the nights.
With heartbeats as drums, we wade through the mist,
In shadows and echoes, our fears coexist.

One step leads to laughter, the next into dread,
Each moment a gamble, each thought a thread.
The mind weaves a tapestry, strong yet so thin,
In the balance of life, we lose just to win.

Yet beauty finds form in the struggle we bear,
In the throes of uncertainty, in the weight of despair.
Through flickering moments, a truth can be seen,
That peace often hides where we've never been.

So walk on the tightrope, with courage as guide,
Embrace the tumult, let your heart decide.
For in the undulating dance of the soul,
Through turmoil we find what makes us feel whole.

Eclipsed by Thought

In shadows of silence, where musings reside,
Thoughts overlap moments, like waves on the tide.
The sun's light may flicker, in thought's vast embrace,
Yet brilliance can flourish and find its own space.

Dark clouds may gather, obscuring the view,
But clarity waits, in the depths of the blue.
With each fleeting notion, a spark may ignite,
Illuminating paths through the echoes of night.

In labyrinths twisted, we wander alone,
Yet find our reflections in thoughts now our own.
The dance of the mind, unpredictable flight,
Can lead us to wisdom when darkness takes flight.

So honor the whispers, let silence be heard,
For in the eclipse, the sweetest thoughts stirred.
With courage, we navigate all that's been sought,
Finding strength in the layers, we uncover in thought.

The Battle Within

A silent war rages deep inside,
Emotions clash, nowhere to hide.
Thoughts like arrows, sharp and true,
Each moment a choice between me and you.

Fear and hope in fierce embrace,
Lost in shadows, I search for grace.
Doubt whispers softly, a treacherous friend,
Yet courage stirs, it will not bend.

The heart is a field, the mind a sword,
Fighting the battles I can't afford.
Yet through the chaos, I find my way,
A glimmer of light at the break of day.

With each conclusion, a lesson learned,
In storms of turmoil, my spirit burned.
But in the stillness, I begin to see,
The strongest soldier lies within me.

Whispers of the Conflicted Mind

In the stillness, voices arise,
Soft as the night, bright as the skies.
Every whisper a flicker of doubt,
Fragmented thoughts twist all about.

Reason and instinct, a tightrope walk,
Silent arguments in my inner talk.
Trust the heart or follow the brain?
Each decision feels like pouring rain.

Fates entwined in delicate threads,
Waking memories, both beautiful and dread.
In the silence, I hear their call,
Seeking truth amidst the squall.

With every breath, I strive to choose,
A path through darkness, I cannot lose.
In the maze of conflict, I'll chart my course,
Finding strength in my inner voice.

Pull of the Inner Storm

A tempest brews beneath my skin,
Chaos whispers where I've been.
Lightning strikes thoughts yet unnamed,
A fury unfiltered, untamed and unframed.

Waves crash loudly against the shore,
Each tide a pull that begs for more.
Fragments of peace scattered like sand,
In the eye of the storm, I take my stand.

Raging winds howl a mournful song,
They echo within, too fierce and strong.
Yet within the storm lies a hidden truth,
Resilience blooms in the winds of youth.

Trust the tempest, let it unfold,
In its embrace, I grow bold.
For every storm that darkens the night,
Will birth a dawn, with promise and light.

Chaotic Confluence

Rivers converge in a wild embrace,
Currents dance in a frenetic chase.
Thoughts clash like waves upon the rock,
In the whirlpools of fate, I must unlock.

Voices collide, a cacophony loud,
Underneath it all, fear stands proud.
Dissonant dreams swirl in my head,
Seeking the path where angels tread.

A puzzle of pieces, scattered and free,
Each fragment whispers a part of me.
Harmony hides in the depths of the fight,
A symphony born from the chaos of night.

So here I stand at the confluence grand,
Moving with waters, just like the sand.
For in the chaos, there's beauty and grace,
A dance of the soul in this sacred space.

Milton Keynes UK
Ingram Content Group UK Ltd.
UKHW022117251124
451529UK00012B/574